Nancy Meryl

No Coincidences "Just Because You Can't See Anything Doesn't Mean That It Doesn't Exist"

ISBN: 0-9859-5730-I
ISBN-I3: 9780985957308

DEDICATION

I wish to dedicate my book to those who have accepted me for whom I am—a psychic medium—and to those who have enabled me to work with this gift and helped me develop my inner ability by watching me grow, growing with me, and for understanding my ability to think outside of the box.

There is a reason I am who I am, and the experiences that have drawn me to becoming a healing person, with respect and knowledge, have led me to accept that fact, given that "there is no turning back."

I address this dedication to those who remain in the physical plane and to those whom I remain loving so deeply in the other veil—home—and I choose to send unconditional love to those who are in the physical and to those who have crossed over to the other side. I wish to thank my mom for raising me with unconditional love, directing me with independence and solid values. Contrary to those who feel that mothers can't be their friends, my mom is not only a wonderful mother—she wins the best mother award—but also, she has been there for me through thick and through thin and is my best friend. I would like to thank my oldest daughter, Heather Whitney, who has supported me like a rock and has encouraged me to continue to write this book. She has contributed her experiences to this book and has allowed me to share them.

Thank you, Sandy, for your unconditional love and support. Thank you for allowing me to believe in myself and for teaching me that "no one has the right to break my spirit." Since this is our school, we cannot prevent all things from happening; however, we can choose a path and a door, and proceed. I give special thanks to Glenn Dove for becoming my mentor, and to Dr. Sheldon Stoff, who has written several books. I am the medium within one such book entitled, *Universal Kabbalah: The Essence of a New Dawning.*

I would very much like to thank Ena Twigg for her insightful wisdom. I thank my guardian angels for enabling me to connect with those who have crossed over, for protecting and guiding me, and for allowing the specific validations to manifest into words, either in my native tongue, English, or in another language spoken only through trance.

"Just because we do not see anything does not mean that it does not exist." ~ Nancy Meryl

I thank and appreciate those who have documented and validated my readings in writing, and thus have enabled me to share them with you. They have led me to determine that energy transmits itself through me, allowing for specifics about a spirit to be gathered, not just that he or she is okay on the other side. I am not here to change your way of thinking, nor am I here to prove to you that life continues outside of the physical form. I have clearly accepted my gift and that I am to follow and work with it during this part of my life. This journey will walk you through an abundance of experiences and readings that have transpired too often to say, "No Coincidences."

By: Nancy Meryl

http://herewomentalk.com/i-like-my-medium-well-done-my-interview-with-medium-nancy-meryl, written by Author elizabeth cassidy from Double Day

TABLE OF CONTENTS

Chapter I: Just the Beginning

It was a brisk morning and I was walking to school at the age of ten when I felt the presence of a male and clearly discerned that it was my dad. He had come to walk with me and connect with me. I was able to smell his pipe and his tobacco. He connected mentally and we conversed without verbally speaking. He had a tendency to walk with me. Even on my first date when I was in Kindergarten. A young boy named Jeffrey took me for pizza. My dad hid behind every tree to make sure that I was safe crossing the street. Funny, he thought I didn't know he was following me, but I knew and let him feel the comfort of protecting me on my first date. I even think he followed me to Sweets and Treats, a candy store in the neighborhood. My mother was a strong believer of the life after and listened to my experiences. She too has a gift, and she has shared many of her experiences with me. I was encouraged to share the experiences that I encountered. It was shortly after my dad had crossed over that he appeared in front of me.

It was as quickly as he came to see me, and was as fast as he disappeared.

I was not finished speaking with him, not in the least, but he must have been for the time being. Could it be that I was missing him and this was all in my mind? Of course, I missed him and he was in my mind all right. He was glued to my thoughts and I know that this was real. I was different because most children do not have these experiences. I was fortunate that my mother was a strong believer of the life after and listened to my experiences, and so did my dad for that matter.

I was not discouraged in any way. Although, I was different from most children my own age, I was full of life, but I questioned almost everything in depth.

I recall asking my childhood friend, Philip, while walking to school, "Now what happens?"

He replied, "We go to school."

But I continued to ask him what happens after that.

Philip replied, "You go home and do your homework."

"But yes, Philip, what happens in life?"

Philip and I were best friends growing up. He understood me like a book. Philip lost his mother in 1971 and I lost my father in 1972. He helped me through understanding the loss. He knew I had lost my dad the moment I went to his house and knocked on the door.

He remembered my pigtails and spoke to me with understanding and compassion. Although Philip did not know that I communicated with my dad, he was realistic in helping me get through a loss that he was closely familiar with. As an adult today, Philip has told me stories about things that I spoke about as a child regarding life after death that I had since forgotten. He refreshed my memory and told me that I was always a very deep person. "A deep thinker." I thought things through and always questioned and dissected each question, supplying them with answers.

It has been known that children who have imaginary friends are spiritually inclined. It is up to the parents or guardians to accept the child's experiences and allow them to express themselves. Children, like the ones I am explaining, are considered indigo children. These children think differently, but are able to look at life outside of the box, even though they appear to be different. They question aspects of our world and ponder about changing the way things are done.

Indigo children are similar to the main character of the book, *A Wrinkle in Time.* The little girl of the story refuses to jump up and down like the other children, so she decides to stand still, in which case the little girl is reprimanded and ostracized.

She ends up being placed in a corner for not following what the other children complied with by jumping up and down.

Indigo children work exclusively with their creativity and view the world in a spiritual context, perhaps more abstract than the norm.

Growing up, I had imaginary friends whose names were Jonny and Pill. Jonny was the right hand and always did the right things and Pill did exactly the opposite, and caused difficulty.

Pill even attempted to drown Jonny in the sink. Pill began to drown, and Jonny dragged him out to the base of the sink and saved his life. Although they lived in turmoil, both got along well.

I sometimes wondered if this relationship were from another lifetime that I was reliving. It felt so real. It felt as though it were a sibling relationship. Jonny and Pill would communicate as though they were twins understanding each other's thoughts and feel one another's pain. I felt as though they were brothers.

Both Jonny and Pill sang together, raced small cars on a racetrack that was placed on a large table, and cooked with one another.

They had intense conversations, yet neither was able to get along too well. They were able to work out their issues with one another and formulate a relationship where they were able to respect one another's feelings.

My ability to use color and write was beyond normal childhood creativity.

While growing up, I wrote a book called *The Carousel* and sold several copies in order to contribute to a charity.

As a child, I lived in a world of color and excitement. I loved to paint and draw and play the piano. Even though my desire to read music was non-existent, I had an ear for music and was able to pick up songs using both hands. I specifically enjoyed teaching myself Beethoven's fifth Symphony and Bach.

At the age of nine, my dad passed away from adrenal cancer.

I recall buying him chocolate kisses for when he returned home from the hospital, but sadly, he did not. I recall my dad telling me that, "we are all made up of flesh and bones, and the rest is the soul that lives on." I continued to keep the spirit that I had within me. I knew that I was a person who was clearly able to use their intuition to discern the correct track, and I always followed my intuition. I had an idea that my dad understood exactly about intuition. He was also a strong believer of the life after death. My dad also possessed a wonderful imagination.

Albert Einstein once stated, "Imagination is stronger than Knowledge. Knowledge is limited, Imagination encircles the world." A person's imagination is their own individual way of expressing themselves. As small children, we imagine our dolls and stuffed animals coming to life, that there are monsters under our beds, or picture what we want to be when we grow up. Our imaginations are expanded when we enter adolescence to encompass creativity.

In school, we use our minds to represent a different way of thinking.

Adults imagine what their life will be like, what job they will have, and even what their house will look like. Imagination can be expressed in countless ways.

Chapter 2: My Mom Visits Ena Twigg

In 1972, my mom went to visit Ena Twigg, a well-known medium who resided in England. During this time, my mom was extremely depressed and felt lost, as she was a young widow raising both my brother and me. Eggs and Jell-O were the only food she would eat. For several months, she hadn't wanted to turn on her radio as she had often done when my dad was alive.

Finally, a few months went by, and one night she decided to turn on the radio. All of a sudden, she heard Julia Rosenblume, the widow of the Rabbi who conducted the Bar Mitzvah ceremonies for both my dad and uncle. Rabbi Rosenblume was a very close friend of Edgar Cayce.

It was then that she knew that she needed to go to England to visit with Ena Twigg to have a reading. Julia Rosenblume spoke often of the amazing medium that her husband so strongly believed in. They say having a spiritual ability is genetic.

My mom arrived at Heathrow Airport in London and went directly to visit with Ena as scheduled. My dad did come through with many validations that only my mother would have known. When my mom returned from England, I decided to write to Ena Twigg explaining my many experiences that had transpired and the several communications that I encountered since I was little. I explained my experiences of floating outside of my body.

Ena Twigg responded with a letter saying the following: "I see a blue aura around you, and you do possess an ability that is 'a gift'."

She informed me that I indeed would become exposed to it and I would help people communicate with their loved ones later on in my life.

Looking back at this letter, I can reflect strongly on the other side—the other veil. This represents the three learning stages.

The stages require working and learning to do things to make improvement. Some of those people who have crossed over have told me that they are working with children who have had illnesses, or some have told me that they are learning to work with compassion, while other are learning to work with animals.

When they were on our plane, they disliked animals. Some have committed suicide and are learning how to deal with problems and face them, or even to help those who have taken their lives into their own hands. Also, from what I am told, we choose the families in our incarnation and work with them.

The relationship may vary, but we tend to travel together.

The objective for those in the physical plane is to understand that love is the ultimate divine, and that warmth and kindness need to be the ultimate focus, as opposed to hatred. Those who have crossed over forgive those with whom they have issues in the physical realm, and they remain in pure unconditional love thereafter.

I have always believed that when a person is alive, the warmth from their astral bodies helps to hold together the ones surrounding them, helping them cope with a loss.

My Uncle Sandy was the brother of my dad and he was an amazing person that inspired me to have spunk, to remain with the spirit of life, and not to allow anyone to take that away from me.

He was like a father, and I consider myself to have been very fortunate.

Over the years, Sandy had the ability to make me feel alive even though my dad died when I was a child. He took me horseback riding and to Adventures Inn almost every weekend. He gave me the world unconditionally. As time went on, a tick bit Sandy. He developed Lime disease, cancer, broke his femur, and went through chemotherapy, radiation, and rehabilitation. Finally, he got excellent care from the VA Hospital. Sandy had been in the Coast Guard.

Chapter 3: Unconditional Love

Being the next of kin, it was a difficult decision to inform him that he had endured a stroke. He looked at me with his blue eyes and wanted to know. I asked the physicians to leave the room so we could chat. I had been sitting outside of the room thinking about the choices that were offered for me to make a decision. The first being a feeding tube, the second being hydration. I saw the doctors poking and prodding my uncle and felt that this was not the way to be, trapped in your own body with people using needles to continue to take blood. Yet, on the other hand, I was being selfish.

If only they could bring him back to the life he enjoyed and the spunk he had that made everyone feel the same, but reality was clear, and it was selfish of me to keep him in the physical for my own selfish purposes. It was time for me to grow up and let go.

My decision was made. I thought it best that he not receive a feeding tube and that he needed to be hydrated. Yes, this was a tough decision, but so humane. I held his hand, thanked him for the last thirty-eight years of my life, and told him to go and that I know he loves me as I love him. The following evening, he crossed over. As much preparation as one can think they need in order to let go, loss stings like a bee. I cried and wanted to feel him, but I was numb. I cried and put the covers over my head and sat in darkness for the entire day not wanting to see the sunlight. One thing that I did understand is that I knew Sandy heard me because the last component to go is a person's hearing. I knew that he knew we both understood our emotions and thoughts, and even though I doubted myself for a week if I should let him go, I knew that I made the correct and unselfish decision by allowing him to cross over with dignity. His passion for being an attorney was incredible. He was a fantastic criminal attorney and could no longer do what he enjoyed doing. Life was painful, and the quality was non-existent. During his eulogy, I spoke to him and not about him. I played the "Sound of Silence" by Simon and Garfunkel.

When the Veterans Procession was completed and the flag was folded and handed to my brother, Jeffrey, I stood alone next to his coffin and felt his presence. I felt guilty that I told him he had a stroke, and then I worked my thoughts by acknowledging to myself that I had freed him. Loving someone is being able to let go. I knew he loved my daughters and was able to see them and spend time with them, not enough time, but they still recall the many pop-up books he bought them.

I really despise burial. I can't seem to deal with an ending. The dirt has always frightened me. In a previous life, I believe that I was in Atlantis or had an unpleasant experience being buried alive.

He was very special, and even though I felt a sense of emptiness and shock, I knew that I would never forget, but the loss would be easier to cope with in time.

Not a day goes by without the thought of him in my mind. I now know he stands next to Heather as her guardian angel.

They were loud and clear and I felt his presence.

They transpired as though they were real, but were they real? Was I just mourning over the loss? How can we define real?

Is real defined as something we are capable of viewing? You see, real does not need to be something we can visualize with our sight.

Can we say actions speak louder than words? Must we physically hear words in order to understand that words are fact?

Chapter 4: Things Began to Happen

My objective is to focus on who, what, where, how, and when.

I tend to omit the *why* component because I refrain from asking that question. Things happen for a reason and *why* is an easy question to ask, but the answer is not readily available, thus we are required to make an explanation for the *why* and *where* while we reflect on what we have experienced in the past. Funny, but my grandmother has always told me that

"Y is a crooked letter."

I didn't choose to become a medium. It happened because it was meant to be. It began with a thought-relaying process that allowed me to hear thoughts clearly——specifically, Sandy's thoughts. They were loud and clear, and I felt his presence. They transpired as though they were real, but were they really real? Was I just mourning over the loss?

How can we define real? Is it something that we are capable of viewing? You see, real does not need to be something we can acknowledge with our sight.

Is communication real? Is speaking real? Stop and think about what you personally feel is real.

My first professor at Bradford College asked questions and allowed us to think.

She taught philosophy and was somewhat Freudian in her thinking, yet she was more surreal in her discussions, allowing her students to reflect on her questions and respond. She shared her thoughts and discussed Socrates and Plato. Can we say actions speak louder than words? Must we physically hear words in order to understand that words are fact?

Is there something other than hearing? Does real need to be confined to the physical, or can it be defined through our sixth sense? In my case, can reality not be validated by specific readings that come about when a spirit has connected with me, and I relay specific details to the sitter? In my case, real becomes a reality when communication is expressed through the mind. Who am I to explain what happens? Let us think about pain. Pain has been described as being felt only in the mind.

However, "if a horse kicks you in the rear, you are going to feel pain."

Therefore, it isn't in the mind. Thus, pain and communication travel differently, but in frequencies.

Sandy babysat for my daughters and enjoyed every moment of being with them that he called himself "Loving Care," I thought that name was rather clever. He would bring the girls pop-up books and read to both of his great nieces. Shortly after Sandy crossed over to the other veil, my mom received some mail, and No Coincidences, the envelope had the return address of Loving Care.

I knew immediately that Sandy was validating his connections to me. It was November, around Thanksgiving, and as usual, I was in the kitchen. Those who have crossed over tend to be there in the kitchen while I am cooking. I would like to say; at least they enjoy my cooking. As I placed the ingredients together on the counter, along came the presence of my uncle, and then my grandmother—almost consecutively. They communicated to me as though they were standing with me in the kitchen. I know that it is important for me to have specific validations as opposed to "he or she is okay."

I need specific validations that I do not have knowledge of so that I can reveal the specifics from the loved ones who have crossed over to those who are here in the physical.

I am just the one who relays messages and transfers these messages into meanings. I only work here.

Sandy asked me to call my mom and to tell her that he was working with his uncle, Harry. I called my mom and she confirmed that Uncle Harry was his uncle that crossed over when Sandy was nine years old.

Nine is a difficult number since my dad passed away when I was nine, my mom's dad passed away when she was nine, when my daughter Hayley was nine, my brother's wife's mother passed away, when Heather was nine, Sandy passed away, and now I am aware of Sandy's uncle Harry who crossed when he was nine.

At Heather's sweet sixteen, one statement that she shared when lighting the candles was, "Mom, the number nine no longer is a negative number because I am going to have eight boys and one girl and that makes nine." I may add that a bottle of Number Nine perfume was given to my daughter on her twentieth birthday from a family member named Carl. He knew the meaning of nine, but had to still be evil and give it to my daughter.

We always had problems with Carl. He was an empty soul and walked the Earth with venom. A few weeks later, I asked Heather what she did with that perfume. She told me that it smelled really nice, but she chose to throw it out. We must be aware that being a medium means being able to protect yourself from snakes. There are many of them in the physical and they are here to bite. We just need to learn how to move them aside. Clearly, Heather mastered her ability to release the snake's venom by removing the poison— the perfume.

While still in the kitchen preparing the food, my grandmother, Frances, came through and asked me to get in touch with my mom and to tell her to continue to wear the ring that she secretly wore for comfort. She described the ring having emeralds and diamonds.

My mom began to cry and left work to come over to my house. She showed me the ring that she privately wore for comfort. At this point, I felt as though I were either mourning, going through the twilight zone, or just experiencing a difficult time from my realization about a loss. This was a difficult period, but I knew in my heart that it was time to seek out someone who could help me, but whom?

As I am writing this part of my book, relaxing in front of my fireplace, a thought enters my mind. Life is all like a cookie and you hold it as one piece, but sometimes the piece crumbles into several tiny pieces that fall apart. I formulate questions in my mind: "Is this GOD's way of testing our strength? Is this something that each individual needs to experience at some point in his or her life?" Notice how I am not questioning this with a why. I can surmise the reasons.

My belief is that we need to develop an inner strength. A strength that we may not already poses, and thus GOD places in us through rigorous tests in order to become stronger in order to reach a higher level of learning.

I do think that without pain there is no gain. Some people do not need to endure difficult tasks to further their understanding of life. Most of us do encounter challenges that strengthen them internally. Is it necessary to go with the pain and accept the flow of what we are experiencing? Should we allow the universe to guide our inner abilities? Sometimes, I think about these questions, and I may have my ideas, but I cannot arrive at a definite answer.

I look at it as something to think about, something we must learn to deal with, and something that we need to encounter to develop inner strength. It wasn't strong enough for me to gain inner strength, but being placed with two children alone, and having been financially abandoned did the trick. The strength inside of me came out like a dragon spitting out fire. I believe GOD tests us, and this test for me was not enough to make my inner self stronger, so he tossed a situation at me. Many of you have gone through similar situations, and it is called survival. I know that having to endure this living death was something GOD gave to me. I feel that he only gives us tests that we are able to handle. I did not know if I could handle this one. Surprisingly enough, I was able to get through "the storm by dancing in the rain."

Chapter 5: I Don't Believe You, Glenn

"They are speaking to you." It wasn't my imagination. It took me some time to get an appointment with Glenn Dove, a well-known medium in Baldwin, New York. I walked into my meeting and met with Glenn not knowing what to expect. He began his session.

Validations came through right and left, and Glenn informed me that I didn't need him because I am a medium capable of doing what he does. I was perturbed and disagreed with Glenn.

But, it wasn't my imagination.

I was stunned, scared, and in denial. So, I disagreed with Glenn. I informed him that I was a college professor in the educational field and that teaching was my passion. I expressed to him that I was focused on helping college students, both graduate and undergraduate, learn compassion, skills, and to teach the children of tomorrow with love. It was my life's work. I had gone from teaching small children to university, and I would go ahead and do it all over if I had to choose my career path again.

I explained that my first college professor in the field of education was Dr. Jeffrey Kane who had inspired me to become a teacher.

He had a different take on education and taught with compassion and a spiritual approach. I recall every step of his class and could not wait until his class was in session. Glenn told me that being a Professor of Education was what my calling was, but just like Ena Twigg told my mom back in 1972, "Nancy is a medium, and she shall not work with her gift until she becomes older."

Glenn assured me that I was able to do readings. He told me that spirits speak to me and I am able to communicate with those who have crossed over.

Glenn informed me that he was a musician, but he learned of his gifts and explained that he continued to play his music in a band but branched out to explore his gift, which is his fabulous ability to communicate with those who have crossed over.

It frightened me that what I had as a little girl was becoming my reality as an adult. I had some difficulty accepting what my gift entailed. I thanked Glenn, but told him I was a teacher, and stood up to leave sooner than my session was scheduled to end. He told me that I would return to him for guidance, and I blatantly told him, "Thank you, but I need to leave."

He whispered, "I will see you in six months."

"No you will not see me in six months," I said as I stormed out of his office.

I soon learned that he was correct. Exactly six months went by, and I was back at Glenn's office. My abilities had become stronger. My sense of smell was direct, as well as specifics, such as names and dates, and Glenn was even able to bring insight and clarity to the questions that I shared with him. I was fascinated with his answers and the guidance that he gave to me.

Glenn became my friend and mentor. I read several books and listened to tapes that he recommended to me. I began to open up, learn, and appreciate. Glen Dove, my friend, my mentor.

Chapter 6: Melisa

In 1993, I began to work with both of Melisa's children, assisting them in academic areas in order to enrich their learning skills. I worked with her two lovely children for years, and our discussions were solely based on education, until one day Melisa when caught sight of a book that I had on my bookshelf. It was a book about Edgar Cayce. Melisa and I learned that we connected deeper than the educational component. We connected with the spiritual elements, things fell into place, and we found that our work was cut out for us in the spiritual realm.

Our first reading was done to connect with red—the first color of learning. I gave Melisa moccasins of both red and white with a soft soul and red strings. Gradually, we worked toward the orange, yellow, green, blue, indigo, and violet level of learning.

I implemented the various colors of the rainbow into my teaching techniques.

Our journey began with a validation from Pow Wow, Melisa's spirit guide who directed us to go to Puerto Rico.

Melisa found a school in need of a philosophy for teaching. The name of the school is called Mi Casita. It was the first school that launched using the CleverTutor method that I implemented. Soon after, I was aired on the radio in Puerto Rico and made the newspaper.

"Mi Casita implements the CleverTutor method of teaching."

Everything began to make sense. My philosophy of teaching utilizing the colors of the rainbow, ROYGBIV, was accepted into this tiny school in Puerto Rico. The school was bare, but it took on color and love.

Our next venture was to locate the grave from Melisa's previous life.

We found it. The readings were specific; in fact, clues from my readings led us directly to the site. We would need to view a coqui, a tiny frog that is heard only during the evening, but we would need to hear one during the day.

Melisa went to look for the coqui, but having grown up in Puerto Rico, she thought it was ridiculous that she was to locate one on the leaf near her grave from a previous life. However, she found the tiny coqui exactly where her spirit guide had informed her it would be, and this frightened Melisa and a friend of the family. As I was trying to sleep, I heard a loud yell: "Oh my GOD!" and Melisa was trying to convince her friend that everything was safe, but being a non-believer and afraid of the unknown was difficult to digest. We proceeded with the reading and the information that Melisa documented, and sure enough, all of the clues given by Pow Wow manifested. Melisa's spirit guide had given us the information to locate her grave from the previous life.

Since there were so many other amazing validations, I will include Melisa's documented reading with this chapter. While learning to meditate with Melisa, I learned to stop everything and let everything pass by, allowing my soul to float. One must always be connected to a cord when meditating. Even when we dream we travel, but we are secured by a cord located on our crown chakra.

Connected to Melisa's meditation and the ability to use her voice, I have included one very important component. It is called, unplugging. I learned this from a conference that I attended with James Van Praagh at the ARE (American Research Enlightenment) in Virginia Beach. He taught everyone in the seminar to think of everyone we loved, whether he or she possessed positive or negative energy, and then close our eyes and place each person on the surface of our hearts with plugs attached. Then we were to envision pulling each person out by the plug until only our own self remained. We were not removing the ones we loved, but rather we were clearing our ability to be our independent selves.

Again, this is not a reflection of getting rid of these people; you are enabling the ability for your soul to be without any outside pressure from other energies. Another wonderful technique that I have learned is the process of energy, again from the conference with James Van Praagh. Using your hands, allow them to part and return without touching one another: circle them around like the wheels of a locomotive train and allow the same method of pulling and pushing the energy between your hands without touching.

As you are doing this, many people feel the imaginary thread pulling and their heat levels rise. Total focus is on the palms of your hands. This component is energy and it relaxes your everyday thoughts. While teaching in this seminar, James Van Praagh chose to play Erin Jacobson's "Feather on the Breath of God." I did have the opportunity to try a meditative technique with my graduate students at the University, and I have included a few responses without names. It was productive, and they did well on their finals in the class after mine.

The tension that they were enduring was quite thick and I asked my students if they would like to go down to a level where they would be more relaxed. They agreed, and it was approved that my students could apply this method to children, and the level of tranquility within the classroom during the day was so productive that educators began to utilize this method before and after school.

Many years ago, meditation was not accepted; however, Transcendental Meditation is being used in schools throughout Long Island and in other states as a mandatory part of their curriculum.

Howard Gardner, who has written his eight stages of multiple intelligence has been given the go ahead to work on his ninth stage entitled, "Spirituality," at Harvard University. This would not have been accepted years ago, but it has been proven that this component is an asset into learning, relaxing, and letting go of garbage that is not productive in our lives.

Many of us define or attempt to define spirituality. This is not religion.

What do you think spirituality means? Try not to answer this immediately—take a few moments to think about what it means. In my own definition to spirituality, the meaning is based on inner feeling related to the sixth sense that has not been defined.

Amazingly enough, the sixth sense is a change for our changing world.

One understands and feels it within them. It is a combined link of the five senses, but the sixth sense is considered an understanding of all of the specifics of your inner thoughts. It is the subconscious surfacing to the conscious being of the self.

Chapter 7: Annie

Annie, I lost you and my heart fell apart, so it has taken me this long to finish writing my book.

Your soul was a gift to me. I learned through you and I found comfort in you, and then I lost you. It was tragic, and my heart was destroyed. I have now learned to never forget, but treasure you in my soul. I can't replace you.

I have learned to think about who I am. GOD only knows how this has affected my emotions and me, how my ability to cry has all watered out. I love you, Annie, and forgive me ever so humble in my subservient comply to differ with another to allow to let you be alone.

When you passed by my back door, my instinct was to be there, but Uncle Sandy said, "Don't let anyone ever break your spirit." I couldn't fight it. It was way over my head and I was in not only a position to listen, but also to be controlled, and I not only lost myself, but my Annie, too.

Perhaps this was a lesson, but a very difficult one, my friend. When I lost you, Annie, I lost myself, and I felt as though I lost Sandy. I now understand, oh Annie; he walked because I allowed my spirit to be broken. In doing so, I lost both of you. Now I feel Sandy returning since the change began in my life. Somehow, my readers, there are times when we must just feel from the writer and grasp what we can because the pain discussed was so difficult that it takes the author years to return to their book. I write about my love for you, Annie, with John Denver's song playing in the background. I am sorry Sandy and Annie; I never allow a day to go by without my heartfelt sorrow, and I never fail to remember to "never to let my spirit be broken."

To my readers, Annie was given to me after Sandy crossed. I flew to Atlanta and then to Daytona Beach, and then I drove twenty-five miles to Deland to find her at the House of Poodles. Sandy told me there would be a connection with Florida and there would be two other connections as well. Sandy's femur broke due to cancer. Annie was born with a twisted femur and both Sandy and Annie's birthday were on May 31. I let both of you down. The pain was horrible when I had you in my arms and you died.

Please, somehow allow me to feel you in my dreams and hold you once again, Annie.

Chapter 8: My Gift

We will always attract people, but what type of person do you want to attract? Misery loves company.

While it took me time to accept my gift, I have learned that it is very special and I will not play with it. I am grateful for my gift because it helps those here in the physical.

As time progressed, word of mouth brought people to visit with me. I learned, listened, and found myself in the middle as a medium. My abilities have progressed throughout the years. I validate specifics, such as names, dates, and smells as documentation for my clients. I have learned to deal with a variety of personalities on the other veil, and they have the same personalities that they did when in the physical.

Sometimes, I become friendly with certain individuals that I meet when in a trance. I am able to work with those who are able to come through and who are extremely assertive. One person who came through was so intense that I needed to take Tylenol for two days in a row.

I learned how to speak with him and my client returned for another reading. I communicated with my guides and asked for a reading that could be done without having a spirit give me pain in order to share how he crossed.

I have been able to use a tape recorder; however, I find that my readings are clearer when my clients write down what I am saying when speaking with a spirit. I tend to be electrical myself, and for some reason, some parts of the tape seem jumbled together. Lights tend to go on and off when my energy is intense, so I ask my clients to turn off their cell phones.

One way that I can share my experience of communication with those who have entered the spiritual plane is by viewing a rain forest's mountains, specifically the rain forest in El Yunque.

While observing the beautiful mountains, you may see a fog form that covers the mountain due to a great storm. This helped me visualize the idea that just because you cannot see something, doesn't mean that it does not exist. This brings us to the question of time and energy.

Energy cannot be seen; however, after attending James Van Praagh's seminar, I learned that energy can lead us to a meditative state, and that by pulling our hands apart several times, like playing the accordion, we begin to feel energy in the form of heat in the palms of our hands.

This energy is felt through our sixth sense. Each psychic medium experiences it in a different way, just as each teacher has his or her own fashion of teaching. I tend to feel and visualize the thickening of the air. It is intense. In fact, I can even determine if the spirit is a male or a female. A softer presence is a female and a stronger one is the male. If it is beneath me, I know it is a child, next to me, it would be a sibling or a friend or a spouse and if it is above me, it is a grandparent or parent.

Another way of explaining the feeling of this energy is warmth between the palms of your hands. This is a gift that I now accept, treasure, and use to guide those who are dealing with a loss, to give them a sense of healing and the ability to cope. It is a gift and not a game.

Personalities both in the physical and in the other veil remain the same.

They come across as either passive or aggressive.

My work is done through trancing. Trancing is when I am on the same level as the spirit that has crossed. How do I communicate with them?

It is as though we are at a slower pace in the physical relative to the other side—as though they are in a helicopter trying to zoom into the earth's atmosphere. Sometimes, it is easy to connect, and other times connecting takes some time. It all depends on the spirit's abilities. Many who believe in the life after while in the physical tend to connect rather fast and are more electrically inclined.

Is it important to recognize life as uplifting or as another day? In my studies with thirteen student teachers, eleven of them had viewed the film called *The Secret* and had begun to implement positivity in their lives.

Two student teachers chose not to view and work with *The Secret*. Eleven out of the thirteen student teachers landed a teaching position.

The other two student teachers did not. In the physical, when we manifest the positive into the universe, we are sending out energy that will be positive for us. If we continue to think on a negative perspective, then that too will be sent out into the universe and will affect what we receive. If in a relationship, whether personal or business related, it is important to think about how you are being treated.

Sometimes we stay in relationships longer than we should be in them.

Sometimes these relationships are more than hurtful; they're abusive emotionally. When we endure pain and we are emotionally drained, it is as though our soul is being cracked in two and we are losing who we are, becoming afraid of our own being. Our ability to be in a good place is hollow. We become the victims, and the attackers eat their way through us and we are no longer who we were placed on this earth to be. I have almost thrown away my gift of mediumship and my gift of working with crystals because I've felt worthless. I was put down, mocked, and laughed at to the highest extreme. I was navigating toward the negative. Nancy was no longer Nancy. Nancy saw herself as a ridiculous person who was too sensitive, "needy," and was unable to do anything.

Using the mind is a critical component to our wellbeing that contains real thoughts and thoughts that are taken over by non-reality. We must defeat these thoughts pertaining to non-reality by doing what we *feel* is right.

Our sixth sense—our intuition—needs to be used wisely. This sense enables us to determine and feel what is really happening, and thus it can alert us to both right and wrong. Do you remember the unplugging component that I learned when attending James Van Praagh's seminar? We need to remove that negative energy from our surroundings, and acknowledge that the negativity we are faced with is purely an enemy.

This is where I urge you in the physical; if someone does not make you feel good about whom you are, and they do not accept you as you are, but instead they mock you, then it is time to turn the page. RUN FOR THE HILLS.

I had lost my soul, lost my sense of value, didn't believe in who I was, and felt alone in a world that made me insecure.

Until one day, I awoke and said to myself, *I am who I am, and this is me. I can't let my spirit be broken, I can't become controlled, and I can't be with a person who is going to destroy me.* Even if you care, and even if you love, no matter what, if your intuition tells you to move on, then you must follow that course despite the pain and the guilt of having to leave. You need to understand who you are for your self-esteem.

Can we say that actions speak louder than words? Must we physically hear words in order to understand that words are facts?

What can we say about Plato and Socrates theories? Should we judge their thinking, or should we make take into consideration their knowledge and reflect with our own reasoning? Reasoning and thoughts are two separate entities. I think, therefore I am. I think I am because I am here. This is the reasoning component. If my mind tells me something, does that mean it is clearly absorbing a fact and conveying it to me? Reasoning is more solid than thinking. Thinking expands into fact, thus thinking creates ideas.

While I know that I see the thickening of the air when a spirit comes to me, very seldom do I visualize the actual ectoplasm. Although it has not happened recently, I encountered seeing my dad. It was a rainy and chilly afternoon when I took a drive to my dad's grave. It was approximately eleven years ago when I felt lost and sad in my life. I was going through some difficult emotional times and I felt very much alone. I know we do not need to go to visit someone at the grave in order to communicate with him or her, yet I felt the need to go to my dad's grave at National Cemetery in Long Island.

I went to the gatehouse to get directions to my dad's grave, and when I arrived, I sat down on the wet grass and began to cry.

The caretaker asked me if I was okay. I replied "yes" and he let me be alone to spend some time with my dad. When my visit was over, I began to walk to my car, but I turned around, saddened, and approximately five gravestones away from my dad's stone stood my dad in a physical form. It looked as though it was a dream, but to my surprise, it was not. He was dressed in a plaid suit with his face as clear as could be, and he had his thick black hair. His ectoplasm released, and as quickly as he appeared, he disappeared. It felt as though dad were there for five minutes. It was as though he were confirming that he heard me, and I was surprised because usually I see the thickening of the air when a spirit is near, but my dad had allowed his ectoplasm to be physically viewed. Apparently, this is not easy for those to do who have crossed over. It takes a tremendous amount of energy to be able to show yourself. Since I was nine years old when he crossed, my mom confirmed that indeed the paid suit he wore was his favorite suit.

My dad had not only come through to see me, but also to show me what I thought I could not see. I saw my dad—it was not a dream based on wishful thinking.

It was reality. I saw what I saw and know that what I saw was real. It was real in the sense that I was able to view him. Just because you can't see something all of the time does not mean that it doesn't exist. I viewed this as a gift since I didn't expect to view him in the physical. I could not express this to everyone since some might think I was crazy.

Now, I look at them with sorrow since they think so much inside of the box. They judge. I am a medium, I have no shame, and I will not hide this gift from anyone. I do, however, separate discussing my gift when teaching an adolescent psychology class or working with a student teacher, but I have implemented relaxation techniques into my curriculum that have been incredibly effective with my students and young children.

Spirits of our loved ones and those who have difficulty cross-ing over all try to connect with those they love. As a medium, I have learned to protect myself from those spirits who are upset with hav-ing crossed over. They are, what we call, stuck. Especially in hospi-tals, it is imperative to protect oneself from a spirit linking onto you and "taking over." Yes, there are ghosts that need assistance moving toward the light. Spirits of our loved ones and spirits of ghosts con-nect with us in many ways.

Ghosts are not bad souls, just souls that are stuck. Twenty years ago, I ventured into my friend Sarah's home in Douglaston, New York. She asked me if I was able to feel anything in a particular room upstairs. I entered the room and I felt as though I did not belong there. I opened the closet door and was physically forced backward and pushed out the door. I know it was a spirit, who else would be trying to frighten me, but I also knew this spirit or ghost was not able to move on. I felt the presence of a male, and he did not want anyone in this room because he wanted his privacy.

Sarah had done some research at the library and learned that a soldier who had grown up in her home and loved his family had been killed at war. This explained why Sarah would awake on occasion and see a soldier in her room. These spirits are stuck and are in between worlds. There are people like Ghostbusters who specifically work with these spirits to enable them to move on to the other side.

My first year of college, I went to a small school in Haverhill, Massachusetts.

There are several stories about people who committed suicide at Bradford College. One freshman girl, who attended the college shortly after Shirley Temple was there, had hung herself in the room above mine. I lived on "Red Carpet" in Academy Hall. It was late Halloween evening when a group of friends decided to visit my roommate and me. We spoke about the Tupelo Bridge that always felt spooky when we walked over it.

Not that it was foggy, but that there was a strange unexplained feeling that each one of us felt usually at night. We spoke about the library where we all spent much time studying and recalled when books would just fall off the shelves. Shortly after we spoke about ghosts, the light in my room turned off and we heard strange sounds from the vacant room upstairs. At this point, we decided to all throw my blanket over our heads and curl up together on my twin-sized bed. It was clear to me that there was something in the room above that made me feel uncomfortable. When the light went out, a senior named Jackie screamed. Her room was directly across from mine. She was spooked because her light went out, and when she went to open the door, her doorknob came off, and when she went to use her phone, it was dead.

The lights eventually came back on in my room. It took about two more hours for the lights in Jackie's room. Years later, I wrote for Pearson Allyn and Bacon, a publishing company in Boston, Massachusetts.

The gentleman that I worked with told me all about Bradford College, how they brought in ghost evaluators who determined that Bradford College was haunted. It didn't surprise me any, but I soon learned that the school was closed and was made into another college. I had transferred to a University in New York, but always remembered my first year at Bradford College in Haverhill. Although I had fond memories of Bradford College, I recall asking my mother, "Why did you send me to a haunted school?"

Some spirits are aggressive and demand attention.

The spirits that I work with are those who have crossed over and are eager to reach their loved ones. Yes, some have those who have committed suicide and others were killed in accidents, but I do not center my work on ghosts. Ghosts are spirits that need specific guidance in moving toward their next destination, acceptance, and peace.

We all have feelings of happiness, anger, and sadness during times of our lives. In fact, going through difficult times in the physical helps us to create inner strength. About one year ago, I decided to go to a hypnotist. She was exceptionally good.

I went because I had a major fear of the dirt. I was petrified of burials and the soil. Trying to make a connection in this life, I was taken into a hypnotic state where I went back into a few lives prior to the one I am in now. I learned of a dark-skinned man who had tossed me into a hole, leaving me trapped there. I looked up, saw my horse, and was worried sick about how I would be there for him. I loved this horse.

Without me, he would not survive. I tried just about everything I could to get out. I kept staring at my horse that I loved, and who loved me back in return. My horse continued to stare at me.

I became weak and dizzy. I could no longer try to work myself up because the tunnel was too deep and my efforts too fruitless. I was not successful in my attempt to remove myself from this hole. My painful death was caused by starvation.

I developed a clear understanding of my hostile feelings for the soil and burial because of my one hypnotherapy session. This session enabled me to forgive, forget and understand all of my fears about the soil. I also have been able to work things through in this incarnation by being able to forgive and accept this person. I was able to do this through my abilities as a medium. It amazed me because I was not certain how I was going to go about it. Since I was able to connect with him, we have been close and have learned to forgive, but not to forget. Since love is the ultimate divine, it is in our best interest in the physical world to work through our issues and resolve them so we can grow and develop our souls. Connecting with the inner self is essential because it allows us to focus with clarity while manifesting positive energy into the universe. Those who are controlling and display anger, loose sight of love. Control is insecurity within and a tool used only to destroy. Hurtful criticism is an indication of one's own neurosis. It is best to be your true self, humble, yet proud—not egotistical. If you work with these positive and non-toxic components, you will understand that love is the ultimate divine.

It is important to admit when you are wrong, know not to fabricate because it will come back to haunt you and take the high road when you have been deceived. Look at it as a learning experience, learn from it, and turn the page. Try not to waste precious energy on the past and do not be hard on yourself.

Chapter 9: Our Tiny, Tiny World

The world we live in is "a small world after all." We live in one country and we visit another one. Amazing how many of us bump into familiar faces when we travel for work or pleasure.

How many times have you had a thought about a person and then that person shows up in your favorite store? Amazing how that can happen. Can like minds connect with one another? Can they connect with one another over long distances? Again, it does not need to be a connection of equal energy in a specific area. The area can range from around the corner to another country. When thinking about that person, you may hear the phone ring. Again, miraculously, it was whom you were just thinking about.

How does that work? Similar to "the Secret," can you really think about what you want and manifest it into your world? The mind is an incredible tool. The mind controls your thoughts. If you think that you are going to have a bad day, then *boom* your day starts with the negative. If you awake and think about how wonderful your day will be, then *poof* the positive enters your space within the universe. Throughout the day, you will observe the behavioral patterns of other people. Those who are positive will be drawn to you. Others who are filled with anger and grumpiness will wish to connect with those also in misery, as they love company. Without even contemplating the thought of connecting verbally with another person, their energy will send out signals.

Think for a few moments. Who are your friends? Who is your spouse? What do you notice about how they treat you? Are they there for you in thickness? Are they busy when you need their thoughts and ideas? Do they care about you and want to be by your side whether they are busy or not? Do they stick by your side? If you notice the pattern of people, the apple doesn't fall far from the tree. We are all products of our childhoods. Parents and/or guardians set the grounds for the personalities we have and are drawn toward. Genetics also plays a huge part in the development of a person's behavior. Personality disorders get increasingly worse as the years progress. They become more apparent and difficult for other people to contend with. Incidents happen where you hear on the news that a family member killed an animal and then his family. Do these people come into this world as "crazies" or are they wired differently? The law holds people accountable for their trials and tribulations. The jails are filled with criminals. They are packed with fathers who have abandoned their families and don't care if they have been left a morsel of food to eat. We wonder how this person is capable of hurting others. It can be mind-boggling. These souls have entered our world with serious lessons that they need to work through. How does this affect their families? The family has been chosen by the criminal to help the soul learn his or her lesson, and the family needs to learn a lesson through the jails and felons. We return to this world because of lessons that we need to learn. We must go through lifetimes of experiences in order to understand the meaning of life, caring, and love.

Many people successfully accomplish their learning in one life, while there are those who will need to be reincarnated.

Then we have three levels of learning when we cross over. Let's look at these levels as steps. If you have done wrong, you will not stand there with a devil's outfit holding a pitchfork in hell. It does not work that way. When people die, they are received on the other side, well aware of how they have done. One familiar person from their lifetime greets them. Then they are directed toward level one, two, or three.

Each level represents a stage for learning.

Level one, are for those who have harmed themselves or others and need to develop an understanding for their actions. The second level will be a learning level and generally they are there to work with those who have crossed over to learn about feelings, teaching those to have compassion or even to understand the psychology of animals and people and they actually work with those who are on this level. The third level will be for those who are spiritually inclined and will be able to work with those souls who cross over to develop and improve their skills. Then they are directed toward level one, two, or three.

Visitation is arranged where those souls on a higher level can go visit those who are on a level lower than level three. Level one can't go up to level two or three and number two can visit level one but not go up to level three.

What are they doing there? They are working, of course. Well, one client of mine needed to know what her son was doing on the other side. It was clear to me that he was helping children who had crossed over by suicide. He helped run the group and direct these children to be stronger people and to develop knowledge about the sadness that their act caused for those who remained in the physical. Some regret their choices; however, please note that what is done is done, and the lesson begins.

If you have taken everything that has been said in this chapter with a grain of salt, how do you view what has been stated regarding the three levels of learning? Do they have any semblance of reality, or do they appear in a non-thought form?

Take time to determine what your thoughts and feelings are. It may be a good idea to write down what you are feeling.

Chapter 10: Several Readings with and without Names

In this chapter, I will discuss some readings that I have done, but I have changed the names in respect for the families'.

One reading was so specific that I thought I would have the police after me.

A close friend of mine from high school phoned me to tell me that he was very ill and his illness was becoming extremely painful. His name was Bret.

We spoke at length while he thanked me for being such a valuable friend during our high school years. We went sailing together and had the same friends, and we gathered at the same parties. His last call to me was two weeks before he crossed over.

Shortly thereafter, a close friend of mine called to tell me that Bret was in the obituary. I was devastated to learn of his death.

As I often did, I went to my favorite Japanese restaurant alone to grade papers. Suddenly, I felt a stirring in the air, and there sat my friend Bret across from me. He asked me to contact his family and inform them of the specifics of his crossing so that they would have validations. These validations involved a delivery of white roses, a red rose with thorns for a family member who he loved, but there had been difficulty in their relationship, a family member's name that met him when he crossed over, and finally information that contained all that the family wished to conceal—that Bret's crossing was self inflicted. He pleaded with me to contact his family. Finally, after several groans of "let it go," I made five calls, hanging up

on all of them except the last one. I developed the courage to intro-
duce myself to the family after twenty years of no communication.

"Hello, Mrs. Claire, This is Nancy from High School."

"Oh, Nancy, dear, it has been such a long time since we have
spoken, how are you my dear?"

"Well, Mrs. Clair, the reason I am calling you is to send you
my condolences regarding the loss of your son."

"Yes, darling, you must know that Bret was quite ill for so
long." "Um, yes, Mrs. Claire, but I want to reveal further and this
is not easy for me."

"What is it?"

"This may be difficult to tell you, however, so I am going to
say this fast. Do you know what a medium is?"

"Well I have heard about mediums but I am not sure what this
entails, Nancy."

At this point, I felt as though I had butterflies in my stomach
and was mentally explaining to Bret that he had better let go of me
if I follow through with his wishes.

"Nancy, darling, what is it?"

Crud, I thought, *now I am up the proverbial creek without a paddle.* I
explained to Bret's mother that he had been met by Mita. The name
was Nita, so close, yet his mother was astonished and asked, "But,
how do you know this?"

I conveyed all, from the guard at the guardhouse who delivered
the white roses, to the red rose with those thorns that symbolize
love and issues between the son and father, and that his death was
self-inflicted, as he jumped from a building.

"Nancy, no one would have known this information, can I
please come to see you?" I thought that she was going to call the
police and come over to reprimand me for having prior knowledge
on something, as opposed to the reality that Bret had come through

and spoken with me. The doorbell rang and it was Mrs. Claire with an apple pie in hand. She had come from upstate with pictures. I am glad that I was able to meet with Mrs. Claire after all of this time and give her comfort and peace in knowing that her son was fine and had crossed peacefully. I informed her that her son had shared all of these validations with me so that I could assure her that he was fine. I do not in any way try to convince anyone that I am a medium with the gift of speaking with those who cross over. It turned out that Mrs. Claire became a believer and was able to begin to move on with her life after learning that her son was out of pain and doing well.

Not that long ago, I met a family who had suffered the loss of their son. He had crossed over from suicide—at least this is what the family had thought. The parents came for a reading together and soon learned that their son had crossed over because of an accident. Their son came through from the other side and explained to me that there had been flammable materials in the garage wall. He had been preparing for a school science project.

He was an excellent student, so the loss came as a surprise to the entire community. The flammable materials were in the garage wall, and in my reading, I was told that these materials caught on fire. The son claimed that flammable material had been hidden in a red pail in the garage wall. He was using a match to light a bulb for his experiment and he caught on fire.

The family had the fire department investigate the wall to determine if there was a red pail with flammable materials that could have contributed to the fire. They found that he had been holding matches in his hand and he burned to death. The case in upstate New York turned out to be an accident and not self-inflicted.

I was asked to detect crimes and suicides, but I declined the position.

After 9/11, a beautiful woman came to me for a visit. During the reading, her husband came through with specific information that I was able to validate. He told me the tower he was in, his name, the floor of the building he was on, and what had transpired on the floor of that building.

I always give just the positive, but in this case, not even a news reporter would be able to document what transpired and what I felt and viewed. I saw the entire scene and all that occurred. His goal was clearly to establish that he was fine and that was apparently what his wife was looking for in order for her to move onward in her life.

One reading was from Israel, another from London, and one was recently in Greece, where someone's grandparents had taken their grandchildren on vacation, all but the youngest child was killed in a car crash. If the sitter is foreign, I tend to speak with them in languages that I normally am unable to speak.

Several years ago, a friend had invited me to a fair in Connecticut.

Of course, I accepted. Here at the fair was a little kiosk where people would stand and get short readings. Her reading was so basic, such as, the sky is blue, and it will be sunny tomorrow. I respectfully awaited her reading to be finished and finally I asked her if I could give her a gift. I had seen a woman who told me that she crossed over due to a fatal illness. I began to tell the fortuneteller that her sister Clarisse had passed on two weeks ago. The fortuneteller flipped out similar to the one in the movie *Ghost* who played by Whoopi Goldberg. The fortuneteller's face turned white and she felt that she should not do this anymore. She wanted my address, but I declined. It is all about the validations and specifics, not just that he or she is okay.

In October of 2009, Annie was killed, and it was a tragedy. It was devastating, and I stopped writing my book. Other components tossed me this deck of cards, yet it was very difficult for me to accept. I know that there will one day be a deeper understanding as to why this transpired. I lost my deepest friend and companion. I miss her terribly, as I'm only human. I wear her tiny charm and key to her heart on my charm bracelet. I am waiting to feel Annie's presence when she feels I am ready. So, you see, while I am human, I understand how important it is to communicate with our loved ones and will wait to feel her thickening of the air, but as I continue to mourn, I will still not ask why because there is a reason for this terrible tragedy.

I could easily continue with the many readings that I have experienced, but unless the reading has been gifted to me in writing, I unfortunately cannot recall what I have conveyed during my trances.

Chapter II: Amendments

People search for a reason to believe.

That is why religion exists; it enables believers to have something to assist in their emotional needs. In truth, we are all GOD. GOD is in every one of us. We are all a product of energy found here in the physical. I view spirituality as a belief within. No one can take this belief away from you, and no one can take away your thoughts, unless you let them. It is all about learning, giving unconditionally, and accepting. Love all for whom they are inside and not what they appear to be from the outside. Go with the universal flow, accept what has transpired, learn from your experiences, love unconditionally, give without needing to receive in return, and remember to be positive and always think love and light.

To quote Dick Sutphen in *Past Lives, Future Loves,* "After coincidence and coincidence and coincidence and coincidences, when do you stop calling it a coincidence?"

The following are thank you letters that have been written to me from my clients. I have changed the names in order to protect the individuals' rights. Others have given me written approval to document their names. Please read the readings and digest all of how each individual has been touched. Again, think, love and light.

1/31/2006

Dear Nancy,

Thank you for sharing your wonderful gift, which has given me immeasurable comfort, understanding, guidance, and joy. I am incredibly blessed that our life's paths have crossed. With love, always,

Julie

Hi Nancy,

I want to share with you how I felt after your reading and describe the solace and comfort I acquired after seeing you. I have always believed, but I didn't realize how greatly I needed validation. You truly have an amazing gift and I thank you so much for sharing it with me. I feel my daddy all around me and now I know it's really true. You brought up a possible pregnancy...not now, but you were very adamant about the next three months. Who knows?? Some of the things you said to me didn't make sense to me like the name Sam.

Later when I spoke to my sister she told me that was her cat when our parents lived in England. You said he had a lot of animals around. J I couldn't believe that you had the names of the people in my life. It makes me feel so amazing by my father's soul and spirit. I know that he was really coming through and watching all over us. I know you don't remember what you say during a lot of readings.

But do you recall anything about the timeframe of my mother's move out of their house? Also, do your students know about your abilities? You'll be glad to know that I found my way home much easier than my journey there.... In more ways than I could have imagined. Thank you so much.

Sincerely,

Lisa

NANCY,

Thanks for the great reading Friday night. It was amazing! Here are some validations that you can quote in your book.

The first thing that Nancy asked was who Joyce or Joy was.

Joy was the name she wanted to pick for me, but my dad didn't like it.

My sister always remembered her saying that she wanted to name me joy.

After my dad died in April, I called Nancy in early June. The day before my dad died, my mom was told by her doctor she had a very rare blood cancer. After doing research on the computer, her prognosis was fifteen to twenty months. I asked Nancy to ask my dad about my mom's illness. She replied that it was her lungs. I dismissed it because although she was just diagnosed with mild emphysema. We were all concerned about this aggressive form of leukemia. In less than two months, she died of ADRS, a rare form of leukemia. It was a lung infection that developed overnight. She died two days later.

My sister wanted me to ask my dad to visit her. I told Nancy to ask him. He said, "I will come to you during your dreams. Lie on your left side with your pink crystal in your hand." When I told my sister what he said, she told me she kept a pink crystal on her nightstand next to her bed.

Thanks,
Eileen

Dear Nancy,

In the New Year card that Tracy sent to me, she included this sentence: "Thank you for sending me to Nancy. Her reading has meant a lot to me." It meant a lot to so many others, I know! Have a wonderful New Year, continuing to bring so much to so many.

Lots of love,
Ellen

Again, Nancy, I can't thank you enough. I've spent most of the time I've seen you just telling my brother, my husband, and kids about this experience. My sister, I'm nervous to hear from...You helped my entire family.

Love,

Patty

Dear Nancy,

I just wanted to thank you for giving me such a wonderful reading today. Even though I cried the entire session, I feel I can move on with my life now that I have spoken to him.

I left your home so uplifted that I cannot begin to tell you.

I want you to know that I have been to the best of the best psychics, including George Anderson, John Edward, and Glen Dove. You are right up there with them in your ability to connect with the other side and the loved ones that we all miss.

I felt so spiritual and happy to re-connect with my family and friends that I have lost over the years. It proves to me that we will see our loved ones again someday. Your kindness and warmth also touched me. I will certainly be seeing you again in the future. Thanks again for making my day.

Marilyn

Nancy,

You were right. Although my brother had cancer of the colon that metastasized to his liver, I read the death certificate when I got home and it sad he eventually died of cardiac arrest. That's why you were pointing to his heart.

Also, the color red may have indicated the blood I was telling you about. The yellow flowers were from my cousin who sent them and I put them at the side of his bed. This reading was so wonderful

Nancy. Even though I cried the entire session, I feel I can move on with my life now that I have spoken to him. You have given me such hope that that my brother is okay on the other side. I look so forward to the next time I see you. Thank you so much for everything,

Marilyn

Nancy,

I just want to thank you so very much for a reading that was so informative and direct and validated everything. There was no way possible that you would have been able to know any of these situations in my life. I just wanted to let you know that a few things you told me I did not understand yesterday at the reading. You told me to go home and digest what was said and then to return to me with knowledge of the subject matter. I did think about it and soon learned that there was something deep seeded to all of these parts. I informed you that I had never met my aunts and uncles and any other family because they were wiped out during the Holocaust. You mentioned that one of my aunts was there with red hair. When I went home and thought about it, I remembered that my dad always spoke about his only sister amongst his three brothers. He always said that she had red hair and they never knew where it came from. Also, you mentioned that one of my friends' husbands died recently. I could not remember that either, until I came home and remembered that one of my childhood friends' husband passed away a few months ago. So you are right. You have to write everything down and it comes to you eventually.

Thank you again,

Marilyn

Hi Nancy,

Don't know if you remember, but I came over for a reading sometime at the end of March. I'm back in town for a bit, and was thinking about arranging another visit, I may not have access to a car this time, so, do you ever do readings over the telephone? Drop me a line with your number and I will get in touch.

Thanks,

Victor

(Victor ended up having a phone reading, during which he learned that his cat was not in the least mad with him since he was killed in a fire.)

Dear Nancy,

Thanks so much for my reading today. After coming home and talking to my youngest daughter Kasey, we were able to put some of the pieces together of things that I just couldn't connect with. The light blue powder dress is the color of the dress that Kasey will be wearing for her sweet sixteen party on September 22.

The wheelchair...my uncle that passed away on June 28 was in a wheelchair when he came to visit us last year. A mention of a lawyer, hopefully, that is something that Kasey is thinking about for her future.

Today you brought a sense of calmness and peacefulness to me. Your connection to my mother made me feel as if she were there beside me, physically. You confirmed everything that I feel—day in and day out, her presence all around me. I am so interested in what you do and feel that there are reasons that we were able to make a connection today.

Please don't hesitate to call.

Thanks again,

Mary

Dear Nancy,

I know you have heard this thousands of times. Your gift is such a gift to us. Helping me connect with the people I have so missed is a huge comfort. I just wanted to keep going on. It truly is strange whom comes through. I was happy to hear them, still trying to make sense out of it all. (I'm getting there!) I am sure you will hear from me again. Your reading was exciting and cathartic. Please accept my heartfelt thanks.

God Bless,

Nancy

Jan. 31, 2006

Dear Nancy,

Thank you for sharing your wonderful gift, which has given me immeasurable comfort,

Dear Nancy,

It was a G-R-E-A-T reading! Thanks for the good wishes. Yes, I know

Stacey will be there. It will be interesting to see what signs she gives to

Seth and Sondra, as well as Bruce and I the night of his wedding.

Although, we have a number of months until then…. But I look forward to all her signs.

Anyhow, Good night, Happy Memorial Day!

Love,

Bonnie

February 22, 2006

Dear Nancy,

I want you to know I enjoyed meeting you and having the opportunity to have a session with you. It was very interesting and thought provoking and I will certainly come and see you again.

In the meantime, I am enclosing my notes. I may have missed some things because I was trying to keep up with you and I know a lot was happening.

Thank you again Nancy with best regards,
Sue

First Reading

Hand gesture—my dad used to do specific hand clasping motion with his left hand when he was frustrated, and this was one of the first things you picked up on. Your imitation of it reminded me so much of him, and I was impressed with the specificity of this validation.

You said he was singing happy birthday, associated with the date July 14. Somehow, it escaped my memory that this is my mother's (my Grandmother's birthday) which I only remembered after leaving the reading and looking back at my notes.

You described him as having a very slow moving cancer over the course of many years and pain in the left side of his head. (He had melanoma for ten years prior to his death, while he went into remission, it came back eight years later and then traveled to his brain.)

You described him in a pink polo shirt; he often wore pink and other colors that most men don't wear.

You talked about him having his own made up language, similar to Pig Latin. (He made up words all of the time, had nicknames for everyone—seemed to have his own code almost.)

Overall, I'd say that your ability to understand and convey my dad's distinct personality was the most amazing part of the reading for me because it left me without a doubt that you were communicating with him. You expressed his thoughts in the exact way he would've spoken them, in his quiet yet hilariously sarcastic manner. You were laughing throughout most of the reading, and repeating to me the funny things he was saying, and I couldn't believe how well you received and relayed not just the messages themselves, but also his unique tone.

Second Reading

You picked up on my mom being involved with someone, and you felt recent commitment and a ring. She got engaged to her boyfriend Mark a few months ago. At another part in the reading, you received the name Mark from my dad and told me that he said, "Mark, Mark, Mark," with a laugh, and that he is approving of my mom's happiness.

You said my dad was wearing a shirt with numbers all over it and joking around that he was a "number man." My dad was pointing to a CPA office and he was an accountant, a CPA, and always loved math and numbers in general.

My dad expressed a Happy Birthday message: Red roses for love and a "J" month, which you narrowed down to January. (This is my mom's birthday month.)

You picked up on the fact that the night before this reading, I had been having a hard time sleeping because I felt my dad all around me and felt as though we were communicating through my mind. Although, I regularly feel as if I'm talking to him, I doubt myself because I have no way of proving that I am. But hearing this validation from him through you was reassuring to me, and it makes me more confident that maybe I really am communicating with him. This reading was different from the first I had with you, because it was more philosophical in nature and it gave me a lot of insight into my plans to move to Australia and the guilt I've felt about leaving my family and friends. I've felt for a long time now that it's something I need to do despite the guilt, but it was reassuring to hear that I'm not doing the wrong thing by going with my instinct.

Anonymous (from Australia)

September 13, 2003

Dear Nancy,

Thank you for having us to your lovely home last month. I am sorry I haven't written sooner but we have been on vacation and also had family visiting. You and our meeting have been on my mind. Too bad I didn't record our conversation so that I could listen your words. I was thinking about some of the things you said about Michael. You mentioned seeing me in front of a window talking to him. I have two theories about that. First, I drive to work every morning praying for Michael and listening to classical music. You thought Michael was musical. He knew I liked classical music and had given me some tapes. Second, I just noticed yesterday that we have a new picture window in the living room and Michael's picture is right in the middle!

You also seemed certain that Michael was communicating the "B" sound. You thought he was traveling with someone whose name started with a "B." I thought that perhaps he wanted to touch base with his brother Billy, with whom he lived for the past two years in California. The "A" sound Michael was trying to communicate could be his brother Andy, his wife Erin (who has been very kind to all of us and who is also very spiritual), or his old girlfriend April.

The friends of Mike that I spoke to after our meeting didn't think it was his new girlfriend Annabelle.

I didn't feel comfortable telling Annabelle about our conversation, although, I did speak with her. You talked about a red helmet, which still does not make sense to me. Could it mean that it was a careless accident? He was not wearing a seatbelt at the time.

As you said, he was sent to our family to teach us a lesson, and it was his time to move on. We all miss him terribly. He was a real gentleman and a fun loving person.

Thanks for assuring us that he is ok and he is always with us.

Hopefully, we will be together when our time in this world is complete.

If you have any further insights or if I can be of help in any way,

Please let me know.

Sincerely,

Mary Jane Russel

Dear Nancy,

Hi!

Actually, Bruce remembered that George Anderson said that Stacey's other sister and her grandfather helped to cross over, you actually validated what Stacey said to George Anderson also.

Also, when she said that she liked the way I did her hair and it looked like she was going to a prom she actually was modeling a dress she designed and sewed for a couple of courses she was taking at the HS.

Anyhow,

Speak to you soon,

Love,

Bonnie

(As I write this beautiful and heartfelt letter, I want to say my reading similar to that of Edgar Cayce healed this client. Sloane Kettering pleaded with John to find out the miracle for shrinking his tumor and for not needing the medications to reduce the pain. The pain was reduced and so was the tumor and John lived one year longer than Sloane Kettering had ever imagined him to live.)

Dear Nancy,

I just wanted to send you this to thank you for the insight to believe.

My eyes were wide open during our session, but little did I realize how much wider they were going to get. When we were together, my beloved grandmother told you to cut a stalk of your Aloe plant and give it to me, the reason being so that I could use the Aloe for the stitches on my head. I didn't hesitate because you told me things during our meeting that there was no way you could have known.

These stitches have been there for over two months with little improvement. In just seven days, the stitches are disappearing and blending into my skin. It is a very noticeable difference because the doctors are asking me what I used. I told them I used a family secret my grandmother from Heaven told me to use. But the most remarkable thing happened the day I got my results for my six weeks of radiation and chemo treatments. The first thing I did that morning was to go to the cemetery to see my grandmother and mother and ask for their help. I now know for a fact that they watch over me. I went to my grandmother's [gravesite] first and thanked her for the talk we had, and to let her know that no matter what happens because of my sickness, she has made it easier to bear, for I know what lies ahead. Next stop, Mom and Dad's gravesites. My mom and dad are buried at Pine Lawn Cemetery. The stones there are flush with the ground to keep a neater appearance. As I pulled up, I noticed something was on the stone. The stone had two pinecones sitting above their names. They looked as if they were perfectly placed: one above Dad's name and one above Mom's. I placed my hands on their names like I always do and let them know that I knew they put those pinecones there for me. Once I finished those words, a pinecone fell out of a tree and hit me in the head. I have the pinecones. Oh yes, the results: The tumors have shrunk, and the doctors now seem to have some optimism that they didn't have before.

Sincerely,
JOHN DUDA

9/13/2009
Dear Nancy,

Knowing you has made my life a much more comfortable and peaceful place. There have been so many experiences with you that have totally comforted and reassured me that my son Craig is very close to me, even though he was killed in a car accident five years ago. I am ever so grateful to you, and so I thought I should perhaps let you know how I feel about what you have given to me. That is why I am writing to you now—to thank you for the many, many smiles you have given me to replace the many, many tears of losing a child.

Nancy, there are just endless stories I could share with you. Countless times you have connected with Craigie, so it is very difficult to choose which ones to put in this thank-you letter. From the very first time I met you, there was a very strong and powerful connection between you and him. The connection has remained strong and powerful and has never faltered. You are truly, consistently, and deeply connected to my son, and that means the world to me. So again, in gratitude, I would like to share some of my stories—stories I relive all of the time for comfort.

Craig had long hair—his trademark—and was always pushing it behind his ears, and I mean always. At our first meeting, right in front of my eyes, you asked me if he was vain and I demonstrated and repeated the exact hair gesture. There are no words to describe how I felt at that moment. It was as if I was looking right at my son! And yes, he was vain!

During another meeting on February 7 2008, you told me that Craig saw a first anniversary coming up at the end of March, and that a baby would be coming to that marriage sooner than expected, and that the baby would be a girl. Again, everything was exact—someone very close to me celebrated a first marriage anniversary at the end of March,

Soon after, a pregnancy was announced earlier than anyone anticipated, and then of course a baby girl was born! All I can say is wow...wow!

In May of this year, I had another experience with you that brought me more of the same big smiles. I have photographs of my son all around my apartment. I placed each with care and thought I have not moved any of them in the several years since I have lived in this apartment. But early this May, I actually did move a picture from my bedroom to my dining room. Within a few days of doing that, you told me Craigie knows that I moved a photograph. It's as if he is right here, which I now know he is—only because of meeting you!

Nancy, as I said, you have made my world a different place and I just wanted to thank you, show my appreciation, and let you know that you have had a most precious impact on my life—an impact that I treasure every day.

Nancy you are a very, very special person, and I consider myself so lucky and so blessed to have met you.

With so much heartfelt appreciation, gratitude, and thanks,
Ginny

July 27, 2004

Dear Nancy,

I just quickly wanted to put into writing two validations I mentioned on the phone to you and to let you know what a tremendous gift you gave to me in doing the session we did together. One thing that my dad said during our session was that he was sending me pink flowers for my birthday, which is in June (I saw you in May). In front of my house is a rhododendron bush that I planted several years ago that has never bloomed. On my birthday, it bloomed for the first time and all the flowers were pink! No doubt in my mind where those pink flowers came from.

Also, my dad said to me during our session that he loves to travel and now he can go anywhere that he wants without a plane ticket.

He went on and on about how he had been to Italy (after he died) and how much he loves Italy. This was a little surprising to me because he never expressed interest in Italy while he was "on this side." When I returned home from seeing you, there was a message on my phone machine from a client who had seen Chris in Italy. They needed my help. (I run my own public relations business) The background to this is a long story, but suffice it to say that some problems with colleagues had occurred in my working for this client in the past. These problems resulted in some very painful experience for me. Shortly after these things had occurred, my business with my client dwindled away. Their calling me on this

Italy project was healing for me. It took me over a month to remember what my dad had said about visiting Italy and put it together. I now believe my dad had something to do with this project happening, and his references to Italy were his humorous ways of letting me know.

Nancy, seeing you and the work you did with me to allow me to communicate with my dad was a gift beyond anything I could ever measure. My whole life, until shortly before my dad died, I could never feel—in my heart—his love for me. He communicated that love and I felt it in my heart before he died and expressed it so many times in our session, and I feel it all the time now. Not just in my heart, but in every cell in my body. I feel loved.

Your gift is amazing, truly. I feel so very blessed to have found my way to you, and I have so many more things I could tell you about our session and the blessings I have gained from it for me and for my family. See you Wednesday.

Love,

Patty Hughes

(This next letter is from a lovely woman with a charming accent whose first name I am at liberty to disclose. She lives in London, and when she visits her apartment In New York, she comes to me for a reading.)

Dear Nancy,

My most vivid memory is that our session together was specific.

There were so many moments of exact dates and names of loved ones, that I truly accepted your gift. Perhaps some of the names were close enough to let me know you were right on.

Your ability to expose dialogue among my cherished loved ones who have departed this earth was moving. There were too many accurate descriptions to make me question your unique skills.

Thank you for sharing the feelings of those I miss and will always love.

What is inspiring is that I am surrounded by them.

Blessings to you and yours,

Janet

Chapter 12: Who are we?

We come into this world from experiences we need to learn, for this is our school.

If there are imperfections and lessons that we need to review, we choose the people we incarnate with. Those people are ones we have already had lives with: "Many lives, many masters." We take our lessons here with us and try to perfect them to better our souls. This school is filled with trials and tribulations.

We must work hard in this school to better ourselves so that we do not need to return to redo what needed to be done in the first place.

We must be kind to all living things, put love in our hearts, and get rid of all of the hatred.

If we are greedy with money, we will lose it all. Be generous, and it will be gained. Money comes and goes in our lifetime. Realize its powers and the effects it has on other people. It can be beneficial if used wisely, or it can be destructive if used as a tool to grasp. Money is important for shelter and food. Money is beneficial, but not a key to internal happiness and joy.

Happiness is internal strength that we possess, and it is able to manifest in our everyday lives. It is the certainty that we can trust and believe in ourselves. GOD listens, hears, and gives us what he feels we can endure in order to learn our lessons. The lesson has been learned once we need not question it any further.

"The Plan": by Sharon Thompson Bishop

People pass through our lives,

Each with something to share.

There is a purpose

For everyone we pass by, and when we have fulfilled

Their part of the plan

They will pass from our life

To go onto the next life they will touch.

If we can learn to accept

This plan, if we can learn to reach out

And take what they have to offer, then we can grow and be-

come

The person we were intended to be.

But if we fight against this plan, And try to hold onto these

passings,

Then we will never find peace,

We will never find happiness,

We will never stop searching, Searching for something that

isn't there.

No Coincidences: By Nancy Meryl

Nancy Meryl is a psychic medium who has had a gift of communicating with those who have crossed over since she was a little girl, but she was informed by Ena Twigg, a psychic medium in England, not to use her gift until later on in her life.

Nancy Meryl's readings are comprised of remarkable validations, shared in her book, *No Coincidences*.

Her ability to connect with those who have crossed over has come through with names, dates, personalities, numbers, smells, birthdays, anniversaries, and specific validations that only the reader could understand. She has the ability to speak several languages while in a trance and has had Sloan Kettering amazed at her healing abilities, which are similar to those of Edgar Cayce.

Her mantra is, "Just because you can't see anything, doesn't mean that it doesn't exist."

Nancy Meryl is the author for the radio show "Here Women Talk" with Kay VanHoesen, and she has been interviewed by elizabeth cassidy from Double Day in an article entitled, "I like My Medium Well Done."

She has aired on "Here Women Talk" and " Unguided Souls."
Website: www.mediumshipbeyond.com
E-mail: nocoincidences23@yahoo.com
E-mail: NMeryl@yahoo.com

Made in the USA
Charleston, SC
15 October 2012